# DUCKS QUACK!

## Pam Scheunemann

Consulting Editor, Diane Craig, M.A./Reading Specialist

**ABDO**
Publishing Company

Published by ABDO Publishing Company, 8000 West 78th Street, Edina, Minnesota 55439.
Copyright © 2009 by Abdo Consulting Group, Inc. International copyrights reserved in all countries.
No part of this book may be reproduced in any form without written permission from the publisher.
SandCastle™ is a trademark and logo of ABDO Publishing Company.
Printed in the United States.

Editor: Katherine Hengel
Content Developer: Nancy Tuminelly
Cover and Interior Design and Production: Oona Gaarder-Juntti, Mighty Media
Photo Credits: Brand X Pictures, ShutterStock

Library of Congress Cataloging-in-Publication Data

Scheunemann, Pam, 1955-
  Ducks quack! / Pam Scheunemann.
    p. cm. -- (Animal sounds)
  ISBN 978-1-60453-571-6
  1. Ducks--Juvenile literature. I. Title.

QL696.A52S322 2009
598.4'1--dc22
                    2008033921

## SandCastle™ Level: Transitional

SandCastle™ books are created by a team of professional educators, reading specialists, and content developers around five essential components—phonemic awareness, phonics, vocabulary, text comprehension, and fluency—to assist young readers as they develop reading skills and strategies and increase their general knowledge. All books are written, reviewed, and leveled for guided reading, early reading intervention, and Accelerated Reader® programs for use in shared, guided, and independent reading and writing activities to support a balanced approach to literacy instruction. The SandCastle™ series has four levels that correspond to early literacy development. The levels are provided to help teachers and parents select appropriate books for young readers.

**Emerging Readers**
(no flags)

**Beginning Readers**
(1 flag)

**Transitional Readers**
(2 flags)

**Fluent Readers**
(3 flags)

SandCastle™ would like to hear from you. Please send us your comments and suggestions.
**sandcastle@abdopublishing.com**

# Ducks can live almost anywhere.

Mallards are the most common duck in the Northern Hemisphere.

# They have feathers instead of hair.

A duck's outer feathers are waterproof.

# Ducks preen their feathers to keep themselves neat.

Ducks use their bills to clean their feathers.

# They walk with a waddle on their webbed feet.

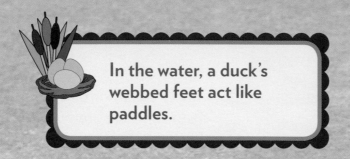

In the water, a duck's webbed feet act like paddles.

# Ducklings follow their mother from the nest to the pond.

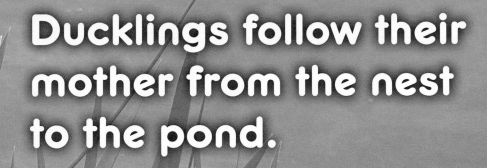

Ducks nest near ponds, rivers, and lakes. When the ducklings are ready, they follow their mother to the water to feed.

# When mother duck quacks, the ducklings respond.

If a duckling gets separated from its mother, it will peep to let her know where it is.

# When ducklings jump in, it's a daring feat!

The mother duck leads her ducklings to good feeding areas.

# They use their bills to find something to eat.

Dabbling ducks eat food found near the surface of the water.

# Soon the young ducks learn how to fly.

Ducks will take flight when they are about two months old.

# They land on the water from up in the sky!

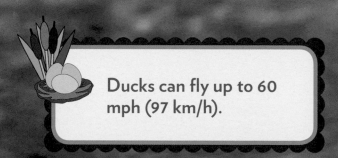

Ducks can fly up to 60 mph (97 km/h).

When you hear a duck quack, you can just quack back!

# Glossary

**bill** (pp. 7, 16) – the jaws of a bird.

**feat** (p. 15) – an act that takes courage.

**imitate** (p. 24) – to copy or mimic someone or something.

**mallard** (p. 3) – a common wild duck. Males have green heads and white bands around their necks.

**Northern Hemisphere** (p. 3) – the half of the earth that is north of the equator.

**preen** (p. 7) – to groom with one's bill.

**respond** (p. 12) – to reply or answer.

**separate** (p. 12) – to part or become disconnected from someone or something.

**waddle** (p. 8) – to sway from side to side while taking short steps.

**waterproof** (p. 4) – made to keep water out.

**webbed** (p. 8) – having toes connected by a web or fold of skin.

## Animal Sounds Around the World

Ducks make the same sound no matter where they live. But the way that humans imitate them depends on what language they speak. Here are some examples of how people around the world make duck sounds:

**English** - quack quack     **French** - coin coin
**German** - quack quack     **Greek** - pa-pa-pa
**Japanese** - ga ga     **Spanish** - cua cua

To see a complete list of SandCastle™ books and other nonfiction titles from ABDO Publishing Company, visit **www.abdopublishing.com**.

8000 West 78th Street, Edina, MN 55439 • 800-800-1312 • fax 952-831-1632